Morning Window

Poems

Bill Brown

Iris Chapbook Series
Oak Ridge, Tennessee

Copyright © 2017 by Bill Brown

ISBN: 978-1-60454-501-2

Cover Artwork: Painting on Handmade Paper by Suzanne Brown

Author Photo: Suzanne Brown

Book Design: Robert B. Cumming, Jr.

Iris Publishing Group, Inc
www.irisbooks.com

Acknowledgments

Auorean: "Morning Opens"

Broad River: "First Snow"

Cape Rock: "Morning Window"

Cloudbank: "Don't Hang Up"

Clover: "Creek Bridge," "Off Church Street," "The Leaving," "Tracing Words," "Window"

Cold Mountain Review: "The Death of Twinkle Toes"

Conclave: "How She Learned to Write (Pushcart Nominee)," "William"

Nashville Arts Magazine: "The Holey"

Number One: "In the university Library," "Last Visit"

POEM: "It: For the Coming Silence," "War and Peace"

Potomac Review: "The Holiness of Words"

River Styx: "Quick"

Second and Church: "Music"

Southern Humanities Review: "New Year's Eve, 2010"

Still: the Journal: "For Symborska," "Scripture"

Tar River Poetry: "Mean Poem for My Wife on Arbor Day," "Ruin"

Contents

Morning Opens

Morning opens
 anonymous,
an unmarked grave,
 stone worn smooth
as a late winter day.
 Buzzards wind
February's pale blue.
 Bare winter limbs
read the breeze.

Story still hides
 beneath the covers—
nothing yet reminds me
 of the dead—
mother, father, friends.
 No scale emerges
to weight the loss,
 they drift dreams,
their faces, places,
 rest easy as forest loam
blanketed with leaves.

Is it possible
 that sorrow can comfort?
The ache,
 a recognition of love;
the quiet of it,
 selfless or selfish?

I'll accept either:
 bless me, forgive me,
it's all the same.

Window

Sometimes a painting is a window
   big enough to step through. It's best
      to take your shoes off so you don't

scar the frame. Just skip your way
   out into a hillside pasture where
      a donkey is guarding a goat herd—

a donkey that wants her nose scratched
   and ears rubbed, the soft inside like
      the nape of a child's neck. A tractor

sits on top, retired, living in a place
   with a view of a creek lined
      with sycamores. Perch on the iron

round of its seat and drive into the past,
   your grandfather's farm at Bible Hill.
      The spring, not a mile away, could

be in a Frost poem, rising clear,
   young enough not to tatter. Take
      the dipper from a maple root and skim

the surface of water striders. Drink
   and Grandfather will be there waiting.
      He is your namesake,

dead some sixty years,
   his rat terrier, Bob, perched
      against his boots.

He doesn't know that
  a painting in the museum
    brought you here.

He scratches Bob's head,
  wonders why you've
    come.

The Holey

Tonight I dream an empty closet—
missing, the sneakers I save for gardening,
the holey T-shirts I won't sacrifice
to the rag sack, Red Wing boots,
beloved and scarred. And the Goodwill
flannel blazer with bulging pockets,

just a wire hanger, bent and lonesome.
This morning the fragile and forlorn
tell our stories; how the years bump by,
and the old and used up, become sirens
of our shrunken odyssey? I awake
to find my closet full, my tatters

rescued, my sock holes intact.
A sense of loss lingers, as if clinging
to the worthless, a form of vanity.
Early March and snow patches comfort
forest shadows. A towhee sings her
morning song and scratches leaf mold

for forage. Pay attention, it's easy
to savor, even cherish decay, how
a rotten log grows the greenest moss,
velveteen and finger fancy, how nostalgia
digests easier than the rush of the day.
Out the window, the world itself a closet,

sun breaks through a parade of clouds,
and spotlights weathered oak on my
neighbor's barn. Across the road an
abandoned scarecrow remains crucified,
straw hat shading button eyes, a penitent
thief, ready to confess.

First Snow

My sister and I rush to the open space
beneath the back porch, hunch together

with our brother's sleeping bag to watch
the flurries turn into a steady fall, as grass

begins to whiten and Josephus, our spaniel,
nestles with us, his breath warm against

our cheeks.... I wake to this dream with
a glorious shiver, mid-August, my sister's

69th birthday... in the dream, our brother
hadn't gone to war, my father hadn't died

and no school tomorrow... a fleeting oasis
without future's shadows... my ghost follows

me downstairs to turn on coffee and feed cats.
He'll visit until Suzanne wakes, then return

to memory's closet where I still smell
GrandSally's coconut cake and fresh hay

and horse dung in GrandMilt's barn. The boy
never says why he comes, and I don't ask.

New Year's Eve, 2010

While riding my bike, a little girl runs into her yard,
throws up her hands and yells *This is the best day of my life.*

I want to drop to my knees and say *instruct me my Guru,*
but why spoil a child's day with lessons. I was once a child,

have seen the pictures, a scrawny kid wearing a railroad cap
and underpants, sitting in a sandbox. Yet, the girl's joy

gives pause. Why day? Why not moment, year, fortnight.
How easy to dismiss a day in our lives, when our bodies

attune to the planet's rotation: daybed, daybook, daybreak,
daydream, day job, daylight, daytime, Day of Atonement.

I return to our loft overlooking the ocean. December 31,
and my neighbors, old and older, wear windbreakers,

stand on decks to watch waves rush the shore. Tomorrow's
New Years and I am reminded of Hayden Carruth's poem

about aging. He realized irreligion didn't keep him from prayer,
and that prayers, written down, became poems. So bless

the kite-surfer jumping waves, least curlews racing the sand
like windup toys, pelicans in magic flight, and my neighbors,

an ancient Jewish couple, who bundle up and walk the shore.
On this New Year's Eve, stare from your mountain top, or down

your city street, or across a barren field and imagine you see
our planet's curvature as it races miles a second around a star.

Feel gravity's miracle and atmosphere hugging you to earth,
as I struggle to make this prayer a poem on the best day

of a girl's life.

Tracing Words

I trace words with my finger:
The day of his death was a dark cold day,
Auden wrote about Yeats,
how news freezes the heart.

A candle is lit so a thaw might come,
self-inside, a stranger, resents the actor
who must pretend to go about business.
No Shiva, no torn clothes, importance

of ritual lost in a busy world.
Emily's *formal feeling* forgotten.
When dementia claimed your mother,
she turned her head from cemeteries.

Two years later, we cast her ashes
at sunset and watched waves roll color
toward the shore. *It's a fine day
to be alive,* I hear my father say...

gone these many years, he lives on,
his attitude a trait to cherish.
Today I have my life, my wife,
and our roses bud in October.

Something arrives at fall's edge,
a late beginning, sumac bright red,
blue sky with clouds that seem clueless.
Could something announce

the importance of now and let
forever sit a while on the porch,
proud of our neighbors' new hay,
the buckskin's flashy eyes.

The Death of Twinkle Toes

It's an old story—just before light
my father starts the car, gets coffee,
heads for work, but he'll be late.
The thump under the back wheel
is his daughter's kitten, quivering
fur in the rear view mirror. He wraps
it in an old blanket, gets the shovel
and plants fur and bones next
to budding buttercups. Then
the tough part: a lie would be easy,
just a disappearance, but that wasn't
his way. He entered the silent house,
crept up the steps to his daughter's
room, sat by her side, nudged her awake,
and confessed that he had killed
Twinkle Toes. As my sister buried
her head in a pillow, darkness cloaked
a contorted face that he wore to work.
That evening he returned, fashioned
two oak sticks into a cross, knotted
them with hemp, and sprinkled yellow
blossoms that bloomed that afternoon.
I remember staring out the window at
my sister and father standing in silence,
shouldering the glow of an April moon.
Our sorrow would be lost to the forgetful
mercies of childhood, but that night
my father stood at the kitchen sink
and scrubbed the hot oil stains from
his mechanic hands that never quite
came clean.

Off Church Street

Early morning streetlamps highlight
   homeless footprints, cigarette butts

smoked through filters, empty beer cans
   at bus stops, McDonalds' castoffs,

crow-burgled. Street corner whispers
   secret themselves above hotel vents,

and alley dumpsters, as trash trucks
   descend on city streets, signal what

can be thrown away and what can
   escape. Their warning reverse sounds

like air raids without bomb shelters,
   just wakeup calls to luckless Vets

who fall asleep to machinegun dreams.
   To them *Mission* means something

other than standing in line for coffee
   and toast.

William

Some rainy nights
I feel a kinship
with city streets,

with car tires
that splice water,
reflecting taillights,

a trashy glare
in which umbrellas
float above heads

like mushroom caps
and homeless crowd
the stoops, the empty

doorways of stores.
The darkness in
their postures

accustomed to
the thoughtless blare
of summer storms,

and the old lady
clutches a baby doll
tight—a blur from

my motel room,
a reminder of
the nursing home

where your mother
caressed William,
whispered in his

plastic ear, smoothed
the swaddle of
his infant gown.

How She Learned to Write

It began on the hospital's 4th floor—
   her grandmother lay wired
      and connected—monitors and morphine drip.

Her mother had a meeting, asked her
   to sit with grandma while she was away.
      The window viewed three consecutive roofs

occupied by a crow and pigeons.
   The freeway traffic reached
      rush-hour's bottleneck early, and it

came to her like a train wreck that
   the old woman who called her darling,
      and sewed her doll's clothes

saved in a secret drawer, would die.
   Her mother returned. Her poem started
      in the elevator, how the crow knew

someone was dying inside,
   about the calloused roofs, how
      hurried cars were stuck in traffic,

how all the tubes and wires led from
   an old woman who wanted to die
      at home in her own bed—

In writing class the next day,
   the girl who wrote nursery rhymes
      for poems, and stories about shopping,

found it her turn to read.
    Her group, who had been so patient,
        were stunned, motioned me to listen.

As she read the poem again
    a shiver climbed my spine
        when she found the cave

in her grandmother's mouth
    that had swallowed
        night.

For Symborska

Perhaps morning's beauty
is thought bland by persons
at the mall, or city traffic doesn't
really conduct Bartok symphonies,
and a homeless woman with child
can't greet morning as if God
birthed it just for her.

Beside the Greenway Lake
a timber rattlesnake's warning
is as loud as a fart on a church pew.
Spice bush and pipe vine flourish
for the lifecycle of swallowtails.
An osprey flies low and swift
up the creek bed, catches a carp
and cries shrill its blessing.
Coreopsis and touch-me-nots
line the banks, an early fall prayer.

Remember in your poem, "REPORT
FROM THE HOSPITAL," friends used
match sticks to draw lots. Who would
visit the dying. You lost and when
you greeted him, he remained silent
and wouldn't let you take his hand.
How you wished to escape the smell
that made you sick. How do
the dying know how to die?

Seated on a bench at forest edge,
I put down your book and watch
cars stop to help an ancient tortoise
cross the road and wonder about
the life we haven't lived as we lived it.

Quick

So this is what
happens when
death flaps in like
a wounded angel—

loss and love join
hands and attempt
to wade quicksand,
because god, having

read Stephen Crane's
poems, takes a
millennium off
to trim his toenails.

Your friend dies
so quick, *so quick*
everyone coughs,
there wasn't time—

things weren't said—
nothing's settled—
mistrust tells the truth
about how long this

might last, and memory,
that swollen knuckle,
only hurts when you
hold too tight.

Ruin

It's an old story. We arrived
at the hospital too late, and my

boyhood friend's wife
beckoned me to join her

in his deathbed holding him.
For a long time we caressed

his head and shoulders as his
warmth receded. I didn't wash

my hands for hours after, wanting
the scent of both bodies to sink in

somehow. Sounds terrible,
how ruin helps us earn our souls.

It: For the Coming Silence

Gravity of waterfall,
    earthworm thought,
        barnacle sleep, flight of an owl,

hummingbird migration.
    It winters with young beech trees
        that keep brown leaves till spring,

is the breeze that sifts them.
    Approachable while praying,
        it is the subject of an impersonal verb.

Do not name it. The space between
    the tock – tock of a rain crow
        in forest crown, it feeds with finches.

It knows the death rattle of a child,
    a dead cell before a new one's born,
        the before and after of adoration.

War and Peace

How often I horrified the war
I was born just after, my father home

from the Pacific, 1945. Yet hilltop ponds
I've sought solace in reflect the same

sun and moon and blur of stars. Vets
still grocery shop in artificial limbs,

and news burbles the death toll hourly—
the arrogant, wretched raping and killing

in the name of some group's god,
another group's greed. Yet morning

brings a flock of green-winged teal,
a stopover on their seasonal journey.

I bow my head in shame and gratitude
for the simple joy they share in living.

Let news sell autos, appliances, chic clothes
while I walk the pasture to Sulphur Creek,

say hello to my neighbor's goat and gloat
on the retired tractor that crowns a hill

in recognition of its service. Near enough
to hear the clear trickle of water, I don't

have to look to imagine darters flash
in running pools. I peel birch bark

and rub its layers between fingers,
toss it to sail a long cascade.

Last Visit

Shadow of the remembered place—
    dogtrot fallen in between bedrooms and kitchen,

no hens bobbing the yard for scraps,
    bream pond, willow choked.

The only well-kept property, the graveyard.
    Crosses poke a sky too big to fathom,

ruled by crows and a circle of vultures.
    Just a two-finger-wave-road

between nowhere and Cub Creek,
    the old school yard fenced in for hogs.

Corn in the bottoms, soy on the hills,
    and factory shifts at the nearest

big town. He doesn't know why
    he brought the old photo album,

family Bible, and his grandfather's
    pocketknife, still blood-sharp.

In the University Library

I ponder the libraries
    I've known sixty years,
        how many fines I acquired
           for delinquent books,
how a few caught
    me so quick that I left,
        book in hand,
           a zombie.
  Heller's *Catch 22*
    and Dykeman's *Tall Woman*
    stare guiltily from
        my home shelf.
I'd return them
    if the library
        hadn't closed
           thirty years ago.
Hardwood panels
    confront me, comfort me—
        take down an old book,
        they say.
I find a note left
    by a student to herself—
        John Keats, she writes,
           died so, so young—
inked in fine script
    beside his sonnet:
        When I Have Fears
           that I Might Cease to Be.
I trace the words
    with my finger tip,
        resist the urge
           to tear out the page—

as if this relic might save
my own lost sentiment.
So many books
I've marked, underlined,
scribbled notes in,
now cave paintings of sorts.
Forty years older than Keats
when he died,
my own *cease to be*
one day a footnote
left in the holy dust
of books.

The Holiness of Words

Soft light on the stairs
coming from window—
if I climb you with my eyes
will a warmth puddle inside

Morning dew on spider webs—
too many to count in a mountain
meadow—teach me the meaning
of *lea – pampa – heath – veldt*

Winter trees, tangle of vines
and fish bones against blue,
you have carpeted the forest
making yourself a nest—loam –
earth – terra-cotta – clunch – kaolin –
marl – taste your words on tongue
and lips, on bark and limbs, in roots

Honey Run, seepage, trickle, bubbling
over rocks, then a stretch of carved
limestone for darters and newts: babbling
that greets the ear or hums too deep
in woodland, taiga, timberland, bush

How many languages have formed you

"Mean Poem" For My Wife on Arbor Day

Whomever writes my biography
will die of boredom. I'm just
a county poet driving back-roads

looking for April. My wife
warns: *If you write one more*
tree poem, I'll send hate-mail

to Druids. Or better yet, call
the tree service and have you
topped. So instead, I write

about buzzards, how ten alight
a bare elm to make it death's
candelabra. "Eert" is tree spelled

backwards; said three times quickly—
eert eert eert and hear a dog
upchuck on a new rug.

Creek Bridge

I return to the same bridge
　over Sulphur Fork. On one side
　　I follow misty current down
　　　channels, around rocks, through
hollow sycamore logs, between
　little stone bed islands. I turn
　　and stare upstream, let creek
　　　movement hypnotize until it
disappears beneath my stance.
　Light on water, coursed with
　　myriad reflections: sky, cloud, flash
　　　of kingfisher, tree limbs. Often
I find a past: boy on Cub Creek
　turning rocks over for snails,
　　dollar pennies, crayfish, or a teen
　　　on Knob Creek watching a girl's
strong hands mold red clay into
　a dwarf, select the right stick
　　to carve out his hair and shape
　　　nose, or a young adult searching
for his father's death, inventing
　cold blue eyes and spittle on
　　a trembling chin. In early winter
　　　a cloud surrounds the bridge.
I remember a boyhood friend
　who'd rather wade-fish a creek
　　than go to a high school dance.
　　　I wear his gloves, left to me three
years past. A stiff breeze
　wrinkles the stream,
　　I feel my face chap,
　　　cup it with my hands.

Don't Hang Up

Only my wife has my cell number.
Yet, October calls with lack of wind,
says drought, not rain, causes maples'
color change, and no news isn't good
news until dark skies bleed. Waiting
alone in a county of farmers, listening
to the roan mare mumble her sorrow,
borrows a day from a life. How many
days would we give for a shower
is a mute question louder than
crumbling leaves of soy and corn,
deeper in the heart than a bank account,
or breakfast made of scratch and gravy.

Such a fuss when so many have nothing.

On another note—rabbits, chipmunks,
red birds, and mockers sneak in and out
of my yard for water—recycled
plastic and tin containers hold
the communion that keeps life living.
How easy it is to become pagan
when cross, star and sickle moon
won't listen and Brahma, Vishnu
and Shiva play poker.

Our knowledge of creation,
self-centered and small.

So I listen to the wind like Thoreau.
What it tells trees
I pretend to understand—
to *make believe*—
a definition of *Faith*.

Scripture

A scripture of starlings
floods the sky like creation,
the bang of them spreads
west against a waning sun.

The news—chemical weapons,
government shutdown,
hostages and death in Kenya.

But on our country ridge
night visits like a prayer,
vespers of towhee and wood thrush.

So what do we make of madness
and grief when maple leaves whisper
peace and the only disturbance—
children called home to supper?

There's no answer but thanksgiving
and shame, how others must live
and die.

Pipe vine drapes the black gum
out my window, barely a shadow
now that night has opened its cool
door at the end of September,
a welcomed guest.

All afternoon I gathered windfalls—
maple, elm, hickory. Tomorrow
will be a burning day before a front
moves in with rain and hummingbirds
drain the feeders to add a layer
of fat before their journey.

Soon I'll wake to find
frost-blighted rose buds
and night longer than day
and our little planet will sail
nebulous and true.

Music

Today music spouting from a car
is as obscure as most passing life,

not a catch-phrase or chorus that transports
you to a father's shower, a childhood campfire.

And a neighbor's grief, often carried
in her eyes, or how one hand fingers

the other's knuckles like prayer beads—
too often lost in your own father's death,

mother's dementia, how at the last visit,
she forgot the name she once gave you.

Oh little sun, flying in the Milky Way,
are you as busy as a single bacterium

busting with purpose under the forest loam?
Mail arrived today addressed to *occupant*—

there's comfort being an unknown citizen,
walking the lake trail as anonymous

as a wood poppy in need of rain,
to know life can turn a curve

without a road sign, and that's
the only tune you have to sing.

The Leaving

The dead return like late June fireflies;
   their random sparks light dark carved
      stones in the boneyard.

Through a wooden fence wound tight
   with maypop, they find openings
      and escape—

earth unwilling to house them long.
   Like life, death's just another journey
      matter must take.

And where have bedtime promises gone?
   The words *never* and *always* that decorated
      prayers are turning and turning into forever.

Oh atoms, molecules,
   do you remember my father's joy,
      my mother's small hands,

the grainy lush of corn light bread?
   Rain will come early morning to bejewel
      a field of spider webs,

to refresh given names in marble,
   water rich grave-bound soil
      that grows plastic flowers.

Morning Window

Sitting at a morning window,
    we watch a summer tree drop
a leaf from its crown,
    windless wobble obeying
gravity, flat surface coasting
    into forest loam. Not
Icarus, not that dramatic.
    Not Persephone's sorrow.
Just a gum leaf's flight
    downward—nine, ten, eleven,
seconds—then, a soft landing
    in the rich chemistry of life
and death carrying on creation's
    genius with us the lucky viewers.

You know the story—*if a tree falls
    in the forest*—and no one sees it,
hears it… if a barnacle dies, if
    a star explodes… if a sub-particle
soars backwards in time…
    if we seek the knowledge
of God, we fall from the garden.

On a beautiful morning when my
    wife and I share an apple
with cheese and bread, our ears
    glued to the towhee's song,
our eyes askance for wonder,
    the neighbor's sorrel prances
down the fence-line, shaking
    its mane in the sun.

www.ingramcontent.com/pod-product-compliance
Lightning Source LLC
Chambersburg PA
CBHW051741040426
42447CB00008B/1252